The Living Crystal

The Living Crystal

*Sri Aurobindo and The Mother on Colours,
Crystals, Gemstones, Stones and Flowers*

Franz Fassbender

Acknowledgements

All quotations of Sri Aurobindo and The Mother are copyright of the Sri Aurobindo Ashram Trust, Pondicherry, with the exception of text from the *Mother's Agenda*. The copyright holder for *Mother's Agenda* is "Institut de Recherches Evolutives".

The Spirit of Auroville is copyright
Huta D. Hindocha, Havyavāhana Trust.

Photographs of Matrimandir and Matrimandir Gardens by Franz Fassbender
Photographs of the Inner Chamber by John Mandeen
Photographs of the Matrimandir Petal rooms by Giorgio Molinari

The Living Crystal
Franz Fassbender
Copyright © 2024 by Prisma
First edition 2024

Print ISBN: 978-81-988068-2-6
eBook ISBN: 978-81-988068-4-0

BISAC Codes
OCC004000   BODY, MIND & SPIRIT / Crystals
GAR004000   Gardening / Flowers / General
BODY, MIND & SPIRIT / Yoga see HEALTH & FITNESS / Yoga
HEA025000   Health & Fitness / Yoga
OCC036000   Body, Mind & Spirit / Spirituality / General

Thema Subject Categories
VX   Mind, body, spirit
AGZC   Colours and colour theory
VF   Family and health
VFMG1   Yoga for exercise
VXA   Mind, body, spirit: thought and practice

Published by:
PRISMA, an imprint of
Digital Media Initiatives | DMI Systems Pvt Ltd
PRISMA, Aurelec/ Prayogshala,
Auroville 605101, Tamil Nadu, India
www.prisma.haus

Contents

Introduction	10
Colours of the Mother's symbol	12
Twelve Meditation rooms inside the "Petals" of Matrimandir	14
Aspects of the Mother and their colours	29
Symbolism of colours seen in Visions and Dreams	30
The Peace Area	40
The Matrimandir Gardens	41
The Garden of Light	42
Mother's Pavilion	44
"In the centre of the lotus there is a seat of the Supreme Mother"	48
In the mineral kingdom is a hidden consciousness	51
Divine Love	54
"You can charge a stone with force"	57
"There are stones… that can accumulate forces"	70

Mother's Game of 'Precious Stones'	74
The Mineral Kingdom	76
Madame David-Neel's jewel	80
Prayers and Meditations of the Mother	81
A Vision	85
The Mother's Diamond Light	91
Earth with its seven Jewel - Centres	93
The Stone Goddess	96
"In tapestried chambers and on crystal floors "	98
The Making of the Matrimandir Crystal Globe	104
On 26th April 1991 the crystal came to the Matrimandir	106
Prayers and Meditations of the Mother	108
The Crystal of the Matrimandir	111
Area below the Matrimandir	127
Matrimandir, the Soul of Auroville	128
Matrimandir's Inner Skin	130
The Mother's Presence and the living Action of Her Grace	134
Encyclopedic Overview of Crystals	136
Electron	140
References	142
Further Resources	146

Introduction

Both Sri Aurobindo and the Mother wrote extensively on the subject of gemstones and Crystals. Of course Sri Aurobindo used the description of gems in his poetry. In *Savitri* one can read about the different gemstones when he describes their nature. There is also Sri Aurobindo's poem "The Stone Goddess". In his text describing "Earth with its seven Jewel-Centres" he nowhere explains what he has seen or what he described; one can only guess.

On the other hand they were also not asked to explain or give an opinion on the use of stones and Crystals. The Mother wrote more about colours when she designed her symbol, and had to select the twelve colours and the meaning of each one.

When the Mother started to have a vision of the Matrimandir and the gardens around it she saw in the centre of the Meditation Chamber a grand globe. The globe was translucent, shining, and then it became a transparent Crystal.

Such a great Crystal was not available for purchase, and so it was later man-made.

After Mother had left we had to ask ourselves, who will inaugurate or charge the crystal, do the *pran pratishtha*, what will happen there?

Time will tell, and it was the Sun itself who took over and answered these questions.

In Vedic times and in contemporary India we find also a great tradition of using Crystals and gemstones. And there is a time before all this, in ancient times, when there was a tradition and technology of using gems and Crystals in still unknown ways, forms and techniques.

Colours of the Mother's symbol

The Mother's symbol represents the creative principle of the Universe. It has the shape of a flower with three parts. The central circle represents the Divine Consciousness; the four inner petals represent the four Powers of the Divine Mother; and the twelve outer petals represent the qualities of the Universal Mother manifested for Her work.

For Matrimandir, the Mother gave the names of her four Powers to the four pillars of the Matrimandir on which the sphere rests. These are:

Maheshwari (Wisdom) - South   Mahakali (Strength) - North
Mahalakshmi (Harmony) - East   Mahasaraswati (Perfection) - West

To the twelve petals around the sphere, she gave the names of the twelve qualities of the Universal Mother, namely Sincerity, Humility, Gratitude, Perseverance, Aspiration, Receptivity, Progress, Courage, Goodness, Generosity, Equality and Peace. She also assigned a specific colour to each of these qualities, and gave Sri Aurobindo's letter of 20.3.1934 as a reference for the colour selection:

Centre and 4 powers white. The 12 all of different colours, in three groups, (1) top group red passing through orange towards yellow, (2) next group yellow passing through green towards blue, (3) blue passing through violet towards red. If white is not convenient, the centre may be gold (powder).

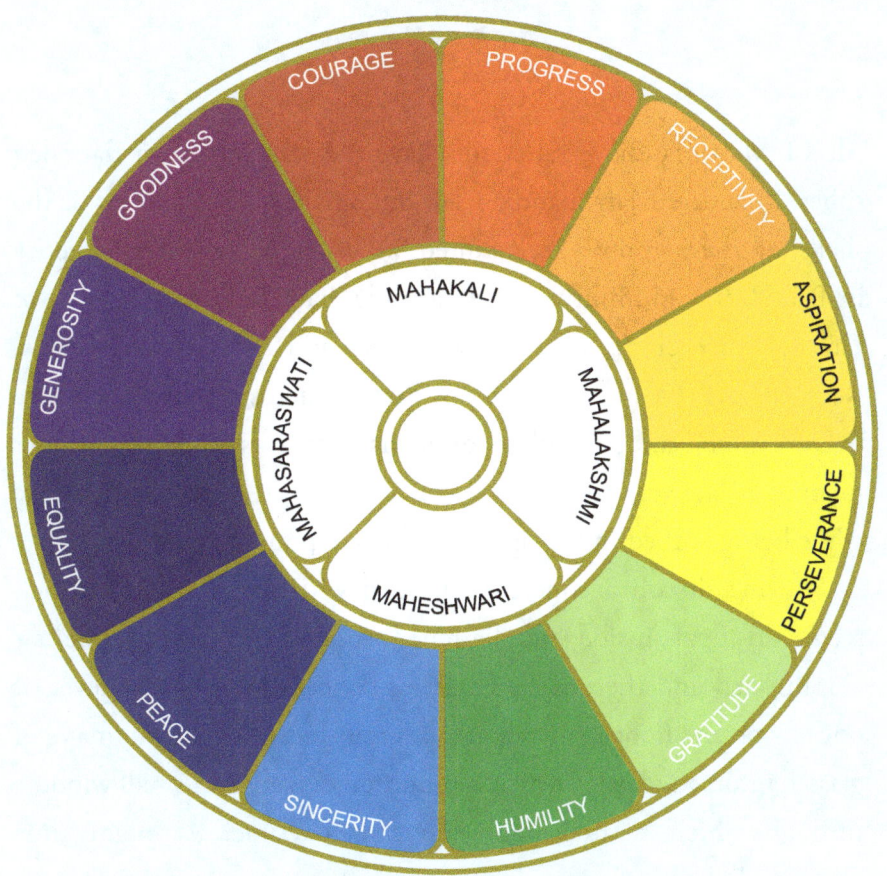

Twelve Meditation rooms inside the "Petals" of Matrimandir

All 12 Matrimandir Petal rooms have the same shape, a flattened sphere (like the Matrimandir itself but smaller). The insides of the shells of these rooms are painted in different colours: Sincerity is Pale Blue, Humility and Gratitude have different shades of Green, Perseverance is Yellow, Aspiration is Golden Yellow, Receptivity is Orange, Courage is Red, Generosity is Violet, Peace is Dark Blue, and the other rooms have colours in between those mentioned above. One sits and concentrates on a particular Virtue while being bathed in the light of the corresponding colour.

So, one sits on a concrete slab clad with white marble, which seems to float inside the flattened sphere. The rooms are air conditioned and there is an object of concentration at eye level (if one sits on the floor). This object is a translucent oval disc (made of glass-reinforced plastic) which is mounted in front of a small window through which natural light enters at daytime. At night time electrical light produces a similar effect. An Auroville artist, Shanta, designed some geometrical patterns on these objects of concentration: a different pattern for each room.

SINCERITY

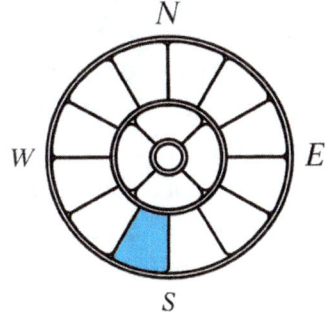

 Every act of sincerity carries in itself its own reward: the feeling of purification, of soaring upwards, of liberation one gets when one has rejected even one particle of falsehood. Sincerity is the safeguard, the protection, the guide, and finally the transforming power.

Light blue is often [the colour] of Illumined Mind.

HUMILITY

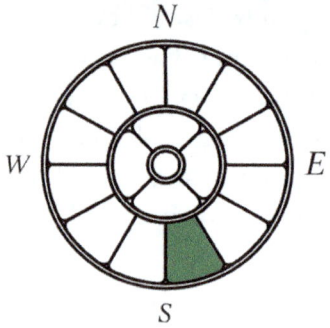

 Humility is the recognition that one does not know, that one knows nothing, and that there may be something beyond what presently appears to us as the truest, the most noble or disinterested. True humility consists in constantly referring oneself to the Lord, in placing all before Him.

Green is a vital energy of work and action.

GRATITUDE

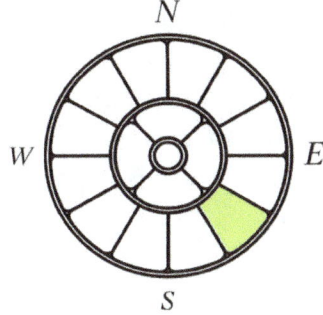

 Physically, materially, upon earth, it is in gratitude that one finds the source of the purest delight.

*

[Gratitude] is certainly, of all the movements within the reach of human consciousness, the one that draws you the most out of your ego.

Green light in the vital physical signifies a force of health.

PERSEVERANCE

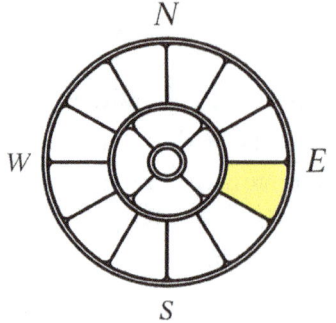

 Be ready to begin again a hundred times the same thing with the same intensity with which one did it the first time and as though one had never done it before. ... If one persists, there comes a time when one is victorious. Victory is to the most persistent.

There is a characteristic colour of mind, yellow...

ASPIRATION

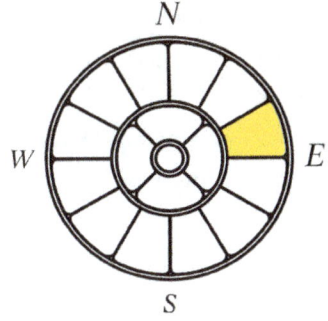

 A spiritual aspiration means having an intense need to unite with the Divine, to give oneself totally to the Divine, not to live outside the divine Consciousness.

The golden light is the Light of the Divine Truth which comes out from the supramental sunlight...

RECEPTIVITY

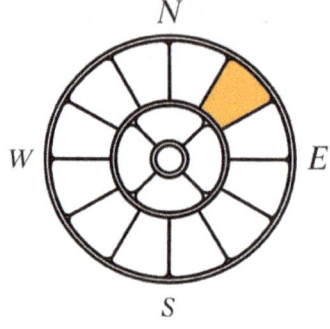

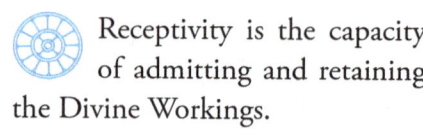 Receptivity is the capacity of admitting and retaining the Divine Workings.

*

It is with the widening of the consciousness and the one-pointedness of the aspiration that the receptivity increases.

 Orange is the true light manifested in the physical consciousness and being.

PROGRESS

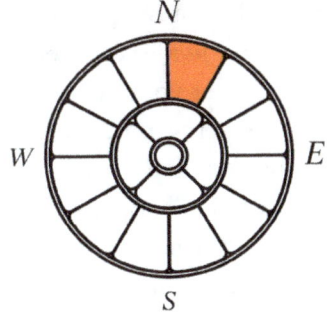

 Above all, it is the will for progress and self-purification that lights the fire. The will for progress. Those who have a strong will, when they turn it towards spiritual progress and purification, automatically light the fire within themselves.

Red is the colour of the physical.

COURAGE

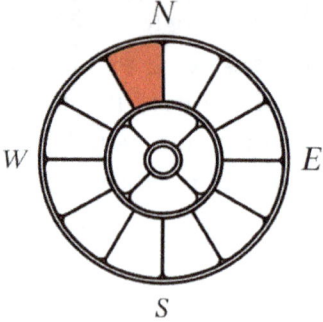

 An indomitable courage, a perfect sincerity, a total self-giving to the extent that you do not calculate or bargain, you do not give with the idea of receiving, you do not offer yourself with the intention of being protected, you do not have a faith that needs proofs – this is indispensable for advancing on the path, – this alone can shelter you against all dangers.

The crimson colour is the light of Love in the vital and physical.

GOODNESS

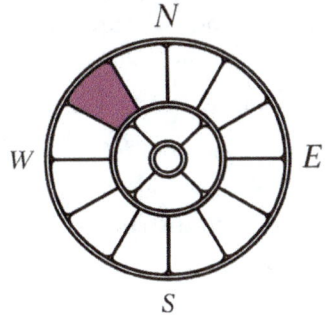

 One must do as well as one can, the best one can, but without expecting a result, without doing it with a view to the result. Just this attitude, to expect a reward for a good action – to become good because one thinks that this will make life easier – takes away all value from the good action.

Purple is the colour of vital power.

GENEROSITY

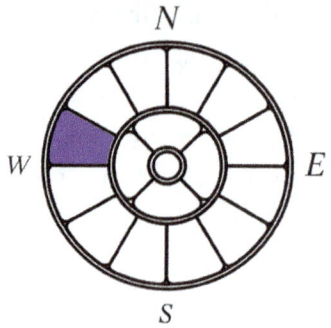

 There is a power, a Divine movement that spreads, diffuses, throws out freely forces and things and whatever else it possesses on all the levels of nature from the most material to the most spiritual planes. ... If truly surrendered to the Divine, [it] will be utilized as an instrument for the divine's work.

The violet is the light of Divine Grace and Compassion.

EQUALITY

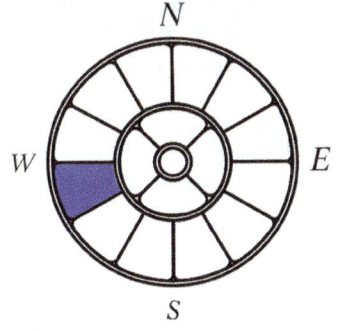

 To be perfect, equality must be invariable and spontaneous, effortless, towards all circumstances, all happenings, all contacts, material or psychological, irrespective of their character and impact.

...there is another [blue], near to purple, which is the light of a power of the vital.

PEACE

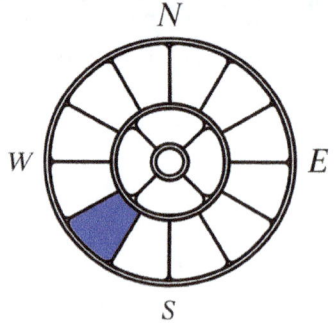

 No matter what one wants to realize, one must begin by establishing this perfect and immutable peace; it is the basis from which one must work.

*

Peace and stillness are the great remedy for disease. When we can bring peace in our cells, we are cured.

...blue is the normal colour of the spiritual planes.

Aspects of the Mother
and their colours

Maheshwari : Wisdom and Compassion

Mahakali : Strength and Power

Mahalakshmi : Beauty and Harmony

Mahasaraswati : Detailed Perfection

They have differently shaped aureoles behind their head depending on what they represent.

The Mother disclosed the colours of their attires:

Maheshwari : Royal blue and gold

Mahakali : Red and gold

Mahalakshmi : Pink, green and mauve, all pastel colours

Mahasaraswati : White and red

Supreme Mother : White and gold

Symbolism of colours seen in Visions and Dreams

from Sri Aurobindo's letters to disciples

Note: names of colours have been capitalized

Colour and light are always close to each other – colour being more indicative, light more dynamic. Colour incandescent becomes light.

✳

As for the exact symbolism of colours, it is not always easy to define exactly, because it is not rigid and precise, but complex, the meaning varying with the field, the combinations, the character and shades of the colour, the play of forces.

✳

There are no separate colours of the beings. There is a characteristic colour of mind, Yellow; of the psychic, Pink or Pale Rose; of the vital, Purple; but these are colours corresponding to the main forces of mind, psychic, vital – they are not the colours of the beings. Also other colours can play, e.g. in the vital, Green and Deep Red as well as Purple, and there are other colours for the hostile vital forces.

The Lights one sees in concentration are the lights of various powers or forces and often lights that come down from the higher consciousness.

*

The four lights were the lights of the Truth – White the purity and power of the divine Truth, Green its active energy for work, Blue the spiritual consciousness of the divine Truth, and Gold its knowledge.

Red, Pink

"Red" depends on the character of the colour, for there are many reds – this may be the colour of the physical consciousness.

*

The deep Red light is a light that comes down into the physical for its change. It is associated with the sunlight and the Golden light.

The deep Red is the light of the Power that descended before the 24th November 1933 for the transformation of the physical.

*

It seems to be an opening of various Powers and the peace, light and wideness of the spiritual Consciousness. The Red Purusha may be the Power of the true physical – Red being the colour of the physical.

The Crimson colour is the light of Love in the vital and physical. Deep Red is the Divine Love – Rosy is the psychic love.

*

The colour of the psychic light is according to what it manifests e.g. psychic love is Pink or Rose, the psychic purity is White, etc.

Reddish Pink Rose = psychic love or surrender.

White Rose = pure spiritual surrender.

*

The Rosy light is that of love – so probably you entered the psychic worlds – or at least one of them.

Orange

Orange is the true light manifested in the physical consciousness and being.

*

Orange or Red Gold is supposed, by the way, to be the light of the supramental in the physical.

*

It is not clear yet. Golden Red is the colour of the supramental physical light – so this Yellow Red may indicate some plane of the overmind in which there is a nearer special connection with that. The Golden Red light has a strong transforming power.

*

Orange is the colour of occult knowledge or occult experience.

Yellow

It is again the ascent into one of the higher planes of mind illumined with the light of the Divine Truth. Yellow is the light of mind growing brighter as one goes higher till it meets the Golden light of the Divine Truth.

Yellow is the thinking mind. The shades indicate different intensities of mental light.

Green

Green light can signify various things according to the context – in the emotional vital it is the colour of a certain form of emotional generosity, in the vital proper an activity with vital abundance or vital generosity behind it – in the vital physical it signifies a force of health.

*

Yes. The Green light is a vital force, a dynamic force of the emotional vital which has the power to purify, harmonise or cure.

*

Green is a vital energy of work and action.

Blue

Blue is the normal colour of the spiritual planes; moonlight indicates the spiritual mind and its light.

*

If the Blue lights were of different shades it might mean the overhead planes, Overmind, Intuition, Illumined Mind, Higher Mind.

The meaning of Blue light depends on the exact character of colour, its shade and nature. A Whitish Blue like moonlight is known as Krishna's light or Sri Aurobindo's light – Light Blue is often that of Illumined Mind – there is another deeper blue that is of the Higher Mind; another, near to Purple, which is the light of a power in the vital.

✽

There are different Krishna lights – Pale Diamond Blue, Lavender Blue, Deep Blue, etc. It depends on the plane in which it manifests....

There is one blue that is the higher mind, a deeper Blue belongs to the mind – Krishna's light in the mind....

All Blue is not Krishna's light....

Diamond Blue, Krishna's light in the overmind – Lavender Blue in intuitive mind.

Blue is also Radha's colour.

✽

The lights indicate the action of certain forces, usually indicated by the colour of the light. Whitish Blue is known as Sri Aurobindo's light or sometimes Sri Krishna's light.

✽

The pale Whitish Blue light is "Sri Aurobindo's Light" – it is the blue light modified by the White light of the Mother.

*

The Pale Blue light is mine, the White light is the Mother's. The world you saw above the head was the plane of the Illumined Mind, which is a level of consciousness much higher than the human intelligence. It is there that the Divine Light and Power come down to be transmitted to the human consciousness, and from there they work and prepare the transformation of the human consciousness and even the physical nature.

Violet, Purple

The Violet is the light of Divine Grace and Compassion.

*

The violet light is that of the Divine Compassion (karuṇā – Grace)

*

"Violet" is the colour of benevolence or compassion, but also more vividly of the Divine Grace – represented in the vision as flowing from the heights of the spiritual consciousness down on the earth. The Golden cup is I suppose the Truth Consciousness.

Violet is the colour of the light of Divine Compassion, as also of Krishna's Grace. It is also the radiance of Krishna's protection. Blue is his special and significant colour, the colour of his aura when he manifests — that is why he is called Nila Krishna. The adjective does not mean that he was blue or dark in his physical body.

*

Purple is the colour of the vital force — Crimson is usually physical.

*

Both [Purple and Crimson] are vital lights, but when seen above they represent the original forces of which the vital are the derivations.

White

White light indicates the divine consciousness.

*

The White light is that of the pure conscious force from which all the rest come.

*

White indicates a force of purity.

The White light is the light of the Mother (the Divine Consciousness) in which all others are contained and from which they can be manifested.

*

Diamonds may indicate the Mother's Light at its intensest, for that is Diamond White light.

Gold

Golden light is that of the Divine Truth on the higher planes; the light of the Divine Truth which comes out from the supramental sunlight and modified according to the level it crosses, creates the ranges from Overmind to Higher Mind.

*

Golden light always means the light of Truth – but the nature of the Truth varies according to the plane to which it belongs. Light is the light of Consciousness, Truth, Knowledge – the Sun is the concentration or source of the Light.

*

Gold indicates at its most intense something from the supramental, otherwise overmind truth or intuitive truth deriving ultimately from the supramental Truth-Consciousness.

The Golden light is that of the modified (overmentalised) supramental i.e. the supramental Light passing through the Overmind, Intuition, etc., and becoming the Light of Truth in each of these things. When it is Golden Red it means the same modified supramental-physical Light, – the Light of Divine Truth in the physical.

*

The Sunlight is the light of the Truth itself – whatever power of Truth it may be – while the other lights derive from Truth.

The Sunlight is the direct light of the Truth; when it gets fused into the vital, it takes the mixed colour – here Gold and Green – just as in the physical it becomes Golden Red or in the mental Golden Yellow.

*

The spiritual Power is naturally more free on its own level than in the body. The Golden colour indicates here Mahakali force which is the strongest for the working in the body.

The Peace Area

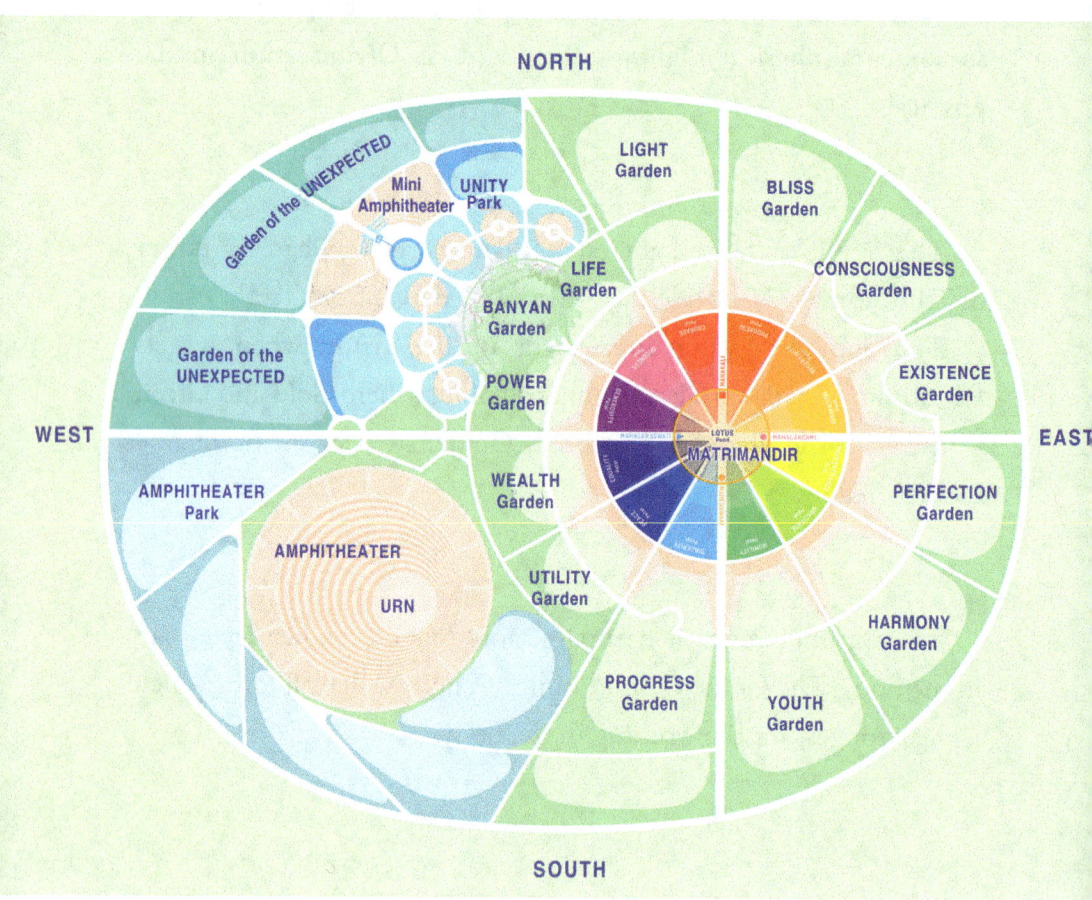

The Matrimandir Gardens

Matrimandir is to be surrounded by twelve gardens creating vibrations of twelve different states, aspects of the Divine in manifestation. These are: Existence, Consciousness, Bliss, Light, Life, Power, Wealth, Utility, Progress, Youth, Harmony and Perfection.

The Gardens of Existence and Consciousness, in the North-East, were the first to be completed. The large crystals currently in the Garden of Existence are relatively new, replacing a massive stone which has been relocated to the Garden of the Unexpected. The Garden of Bliss was created according to one design and is now undergoing revision.

The Garden of Progress, in the South, was the fourth to be made. The Gardens of Life and Power, near the Banyan Tree, were recently completed, and the Garden of Wealth is in full construction mode.

The newest completed garden is the Garden of Light.

The Garden of Light

Together with the Garden of Bliss, the Garden of Light faces the north pillar entrance of the Matrimandir, that of Mahakali. The corresponding Petal meditation rooms are Progress and Courage.

In this Garden a long, straight, raylike marble water channel carries clear water continuously from the far edge of the garden towards the Matrimandir.

The flower chosen by the Mother for the Garden of Light is the hibiscus named by Her "Light of the purified Power", and her commentary on its significance is: "Of an irresistible simplicity in its power solely consecrated to the Divine."

Mother's Pavilion

The Mother's conversation with Huta, 1965

"Ah! Now the Mother Pavilion. This will be a separate island surrounded by a lake, tall trees, gardens with various kinds of flowers. I especially want the creepers of red hibiscus (Power) upon the outer dome of the Mother's Pavilion. They will look like living jewels against the white marble. There will be rockeries in Japanese style, varieties of cactus, small waterfalls, small pools with lilies, lotuses, small bridges, various kinds of fountains and marble statues – one of them will be Shiva in deep trance. From his matted hair flows the water like a fountain ..."

She continued:

"There will be only one entrance. I want precious, semi-precious and artificial stones to be laid from the gate to the Mother's Pavilion in gradations, because they are full of meaning."

The Mother revealed many interesting things about the precious and semi-precious stones.

According to her, Topaz corresponds to Jupiter, the God of benevolence. It is top-most and has tremendous power over other planets.

In 1965 the Mother asked me to wear Topaz, because she explained that the mounts of Jupiter on both my hands are very good and that I derive energy from Sri Aurobindo's Jupiter which is extremely powerful. For Amethyst she has revealed that it has a power of protection.

The Diamond represents the Mother's Light and Consciousness. Also there are Pearls, Corals, Emeralds, Rubies and other numerous attractive multicoloured stones. They have different cuts, qualities and symbols.

The stones have their own individuality and characteristic. They are conscious, sensitive, receptive and full of energetic vibrations. They hold in them the occult and spiritual power. Their influence and magnetic effect on human life are unique.

Here is the sketch of the Mother's Pavilion done by the Mother:

She told me:

"The Pavilion will be in white marble and will have three storeys. The ground floor will be a huge marble hall – nothing material is to be kept in it except an arrangement by which there will be a perpetual flame representing the Immortal Flame of the Supreme Truth.

This flame will burn in a lotus built in the centre of Sri Aurobindo's symbol and my symbol combined, in a design made of pure gold. The Supreme Truth will be invoked in it."

Huta, *The Spirit of Auroville*

In the centre of the lotus there is a seat of the Supreme Mother

(Huta:) The Mother had made a sketch depicting the lotus to receive the soil from different nations and the Indian States at the Foundation Ceremony of Auroville. It was given to me by her grand-daughter, Pourna Prema.

The sketch represents the Mother's occult vision. She very much wanted a lotus like this as a foundation structure at the Centre of Auroville for February 28th, 1968. ... Her sketch indicates a round base showing Sri Aurobindo's and the Mother's symbols combined, and a square pedestal above the base. According to Sri Aurobindo, the square signifies "Supramental Perfection". The height of the structure from the base to the top-most of the petals is marked by the Mother as 1.65 metres, her own height. At the top are four lotus petals, signifying the four Powers of the Supreme Mother,

Maheshwari, Mahakali, Mahalakshmi, Mahasaraswati. Around these four petals are twelve more signifying the twelve Attributes of the four Powers.

The Mother also indicated the colour of the lotus: *"Marbre rose ou blanc"* – pink or white marble.

In the centre of the lotus there is a seat of the Supreme Mother.

Sri Aurobindo has written about the white lotus:

It is the Mother's flower, the flower of divine Consciousness.

Huta, *The Spirit of Auroville*

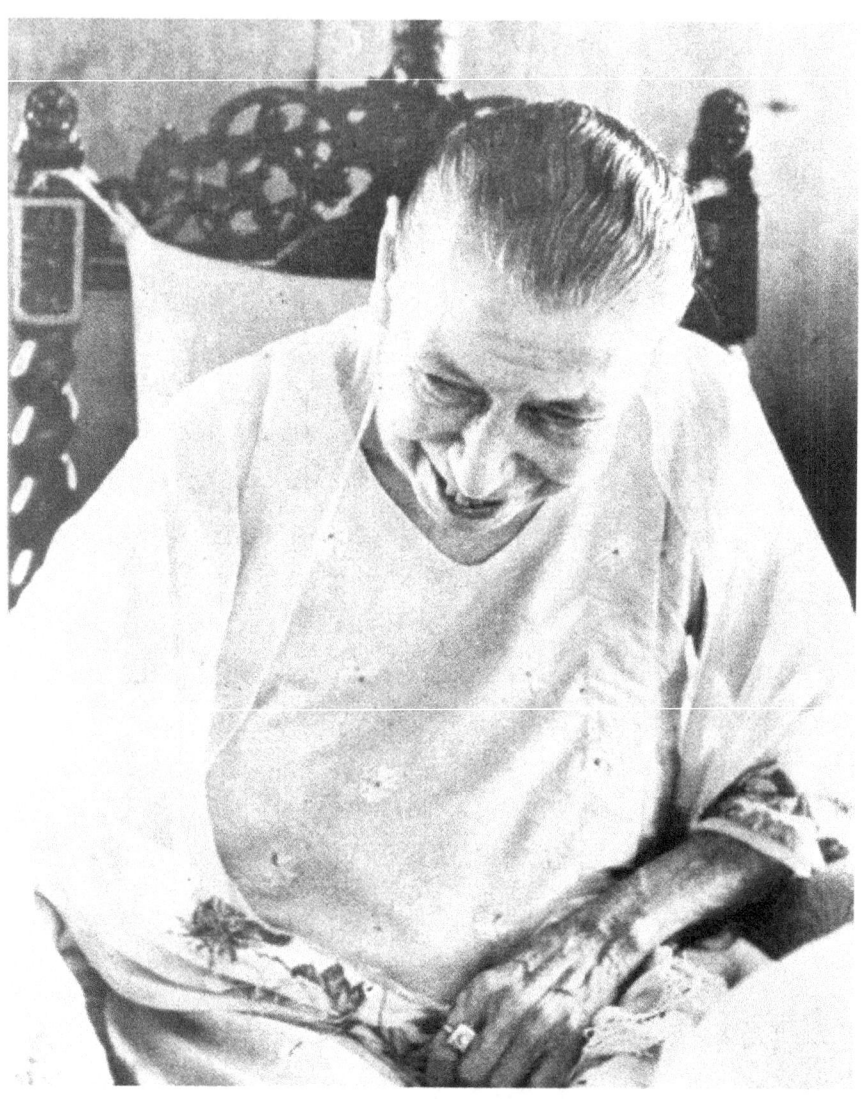

Mother is wearing on her left index finger a golden ring with Sri Aurobindo's symbol and a diamond in the centre.

In the mineral kingdom is a hidden consciousness

Mother, here Sri Aurobindo writes: "the dumb secrecy of her inconscience". Why her "inconscience"?

Whose inconscience?

Nature's.

No, Nature is not unconscious, but she has an *appearance* of unconsciousness. It began with the inconscience, but in the depths of the inconscience there was consciousness, and this consciousness is gradually developing. For instance, mineral nature, stones, earth, metals, water, air, all this seems to be quite unconscious, although if one observes closely... And now science is discovering that this is only an appearance, that all this is only concentrated energy,

and of course it is a conscious force which has produced all this. But apparently, when we see a rock, we don't think it is conscious, it does not give the impression of being conscious, it seems to be altogether unconscious.

It is the appearance that is inconscient. It becomes more and more conscious. Even in the mineral kingdom there are phenomena which reveal a hidden consciousness, like certain crystals, for instance. If you see with what precision, what exactitude and harmony they are formed, if you are in the least open, you are bound to feel that behind there's a consciousness at work, that this cannot be the result of unconscious chance.

Have you seen rock-crystals?... You have never seen a rock-crystal?

Yes.

It is pretty, isn't it? It is something very artistic.

And the movements of the sea, the movements of the air, of the wind, one can't help feeling that behind there is a consciousness or even many consciousnesses at work. In fact, it is like that. Only the most superficial appearance is inconscient.

Questions and Answers 1958

Divine Love

(Student:) You say, "Love is everywhere. Its movement is there in plants, perhaps in the very stones..." If there is love in a stone, how can one see it?

(Mother:) Perhaps the different elements constituting the stone are coordinated by the spark of love. I am sure that when the Divine Love descended into Matter, this Matter was quite unconscious, it had absolutely no form; it may even be said that forms in general are the result of the effort of Love to bring consciousness into Matter. If one of you (I have my doubts, but still) went down into the Inconscient, what is called the pure Inconscient, you would realise what it is. A stone will seem to you a marvellously conscious object in comparison. You speak disdainfully of a stone because you have just a wee bit more consciousness than it has, but the difference between the consciousness of the stone and the total Inconscient is perhaps greater than that between the stone and you. And the coming out of the Inconscient is due exclusively to the sacrifice of the Divine, to this descent of divine Love into the Inconscient. Consequently, when I said "perhaps in the stone", I could have removed the "perhaps" — I can assert that even in the stone it is there. There would be nothing, neither stone nor metal nor any organisation of atoms without this presence of divine Love.

Most people say there is "consciousness" when they begin to think — when one doesn't think one is not conscious. But plants are perfectly conscious and yet they do not think. They have very precise sensations which are the expression of a consciousness, but they do not think. Animals begin to think and their reactions are much more complex. But both plants and animals are conscious. One can be conscious of a sensation without having the least thought.

Questions and Answers 1951

You can charge a stone with force

Sweet Mother, last time you said that stones have a kind of receptivity.
Yes.
What kind of receptivity?

Perhaps they have even something resembling sensitivity. For instance, if you have a precious stone – precious stones of course have a much more perfect structure than ordinary ones, and with perfection consciousness increases – but if you take a precious stone, you can charge it with consciousness and force; you can put, accumulate force within it. So it is receptive, otherwise it will not receive it, it could not keep it. You can charge it. As one charges an electric battery, you can charge a stone with force, put conscious force into a stone; it keeps it and can transmit it to someone. Therefore this stone has a receptivity. Otherwise it could not do this.

Flowers are extremely receptive. All the flowers to which I have given a significance receive exactly the force I put into them and transmit it. People don't always receive it because most of the time they are less receptive than the flower, and they waste the force that has been put in it through their unconsciousness and lack of receptivity. But the force is there, and the flower receives it wonderfully.

I knew this a very long time ago. Fifty years ago there was that occultist who later gave me lessons in occultism for two years. His wife was a wonderful clairvoyant and had an absolutely remarkable capacity – precisely – of transmitting forces. They lived in Tlemcen. I was in Paris. I used to correspond with them. I had not yet met them at all. And then, one day, she sent me in a letter petals of the pomegranate flower, "Divine's Love".

At that time I had not given the meaning to the flower. She sent me petals of pomegranate flowers telling me that these petals were bringing me her protection and force.

Now, at that time I used to wear my watch on a chain. Wrist-watches were not known then or there were very few. And there was also a small eighteenth century magnifying-glass. It was quite small, as large as this *(gesture)*, and it had two lenses, you see, like all reading-glasses; there were two lenses mounted on a small golden frame, and it was hanging from my chain. Now, between the two glasses I put these petals, and I used to carry this about with me always because I wanted to keep it with me; you see, I trusted this lady and knew she had power. I wanted to keep this with me,

Intensity of consciousness in the full Supramental Light
It is radiant and shining in order to illumine the world.
Helianthus. Yellow, double.

and I always felt a kind of energy, warmth, confidence, force which came from that thing.... I did not think about it, you see, but I felt it like that.

And then, one day, suddenly I felt quite depleted, as though a support that was there had gone. Something very unpleasant. I said, "It is strange; what has happened? Nothing really unpleasant has happened to me. Why do I feel like this, so empty, emptied of energy?" And in the evening, when I took off my watch and chain, I noticed that one of the small glasses had come off and all the petals were gone. There was not one petal left. Then I really knew that they carried a considerable charge of power, for I had felt the difference without even knowing the reason. I didn't know the reason and yet it had made a considerable difference. So it was after this that I saw how one could use flowers by charging them with forces. They are extremely receptive.

(A noise continues.) Now that's enough, I suppose? Enough of that noise!

Another question? *(A loud noise – Boom!)*

Do flowers retain the force always, even when they decay?

Decay? No, my child; when they dry up, yes. Decayed flowers are just nothing. A decomposition takes place, so the thing disappears. Perhaps it brings energy to the soil, that's quite possible; but still, when it decays it is good only to make manure to grow other flowers. But if it dries up, it is preserved, it can remain for quite a long time.

Those small packets which I give on Kali Puja day are made to be preserved for one year. For a year they keep their force intact and I renew them every year to make sure that... I know that there isn't one in ten among you who makes a proper use of it... but still, I give it on the off-chance for those who know how to use it. It is prepared to keep the force for one year. And when I give the new one, you can dispose of the other. Usually it has fallen to dust. Not always.... But these little packets keep their charge of force exactly for one year.

Sweet Mother, what should we do with the flowers which you give us every day?

Flowers? You ought to keep them as long as they are fresh, and when they are no longer so, you must collect them and give them to the gardener (any gardener you know), so that he can put them in the earth to produce other flowers. Yes, one must give back to the earth what it has given us, for otherwise it will become poor.

Mother, certain flowers come in a particular season; does this mean that during that season a greater force is at work?

This is a question which is difficult to answer. But I have made a rather interesting experiment in this way.

I don't know if you remember – if you were there – if you remember the time when flowers used to be counted; you see, it was a kind of agreement between me and Nature. To each of these flowers I had given a particular value, not only its significance but its value. For example – it was understood – I had made an agreement with Nature. Take, for instance, the "transformation" flowers; note that if one is quite attentive, one will see that in different seasons one flower is replaced by another with a similar or close significance, and you can go all round the year in this way – if you know how to make use of things! There are also permanent things which are always there.... But flowers, for example, like the "transformation" flowers, have a season, quite a long one, but still a season. The "realisation" flower has a fairly long season, but it doesn't come at the same time as the "transformation" flower.... They... how shall I put it?... overlap. One begins before the other finishes. But the seasons when they come abundantly are not the same, and all flowers are like that. Yes, it is arranged. This answers your question, doesn't it? These are shades in the meaning and it is possible that some seasons are more favourable; one may lay greater stress on one movement than on another.

But each of these flowers had a numerical value, and I used to write it down; I had them counted, because I was noting the numerical value. I stopped when my pages... I had long pages like

Spiritual power of healing
Opening and receptivity to the divine influence.
Petrea volubilis. Violet

this, you see *(Mother stretches out her arms to indicate the length of the pages)*, because I was totalling up the numerical values. I had my reasons for it, it was not just like that.... I did a great deal of work with it.... I had to stop because it was taking too much time. You see, when I had to write figures on a paper at least as long as this, and then later, suddenly it had to be still bigger, it was impossible! *(Mother stretches out her arms again.)* So I had to stop. I stopped because of this. But not only did I have a numerical value and did some work upon it, there was also the meaning of the flower.

Well, it was an agreement like this: the numerical value corresponded to something that it was understood Nature would give me for my work, but the significance of the flower also was something agreed upon between me and Nature. For example, take "transformation". When there was a computation – it was sometimes by thousands during the season, you know – well, it represented (it was an understanding with Nature) that the same number of men would be transformed.... And it was even much better than this. It was that when I gave somebody one, two, three, four, five flowers, I gave him at the same time the power to transform as many elements within him. But naturally, for this to work in all sincerity, it had not to pass through the head; because when their head starts working – not always in the right way – men spoil everything. That is why I never used to say anything about this.

It was the same thing for all flowers, "aspiration", for example: the "aspiration" flowers which used to come in large basketfuls, you know; there were thousands and thousands of them, all counted.... Well, each one represented an aspiration; and even now, sometimes, when I have flowers like "prayer"... I have at times told you when I distribute "prayer" flowers, "it is a prayer. Be careful, this prayer is granted." I did that, you remember, don't you? And I told you, "Take care of your 'prayer'. Pray only for what you want should be! Take great care! Because this prayer is granted. I give the flower, but at the same time the possibility of [...]¹ the prayer you will make. Well, it will be granted." It was very interesting, in the sense that I always used to tell Nature, "You know, if you don't want me to have these things, you need not give them to me." There were fluctuations, there were times when things came in abundance, when I insisted; there were times when they stopped abruptly, why one couldn't tell, one did not understand.... She did not agree to give us... Other things, on the contrary, she gave in great abundance.

But all this is what goes on behind the scene, behind the stage.

When we have a ring or some ornament with your image, does it give us protection?

My child, all I can hear is the fireworks!

---

¹ Word missing in transcript.

(The child repeats the question.)

It depends above all on what you think about it! Something I give you with my own hands – there I put in something; but if it is of your own choice that you have taken a ring or a portrait, something, and you wear it... if you have the trust, the faith that it protects you, it protects you. When I give it, I give it with something completely different from the thing itself. It can contain this thing if I put it in, but if I don't, it does not contain it.

Sri Aurobindo used to say, you know, that to wear a ring with his portrait and think that it protects you, is a superstition! He would tell you it is a superstition! That is, it depends on what you think about it. It depends solely on what you think about it. If he had given you a ring, saying, "Wear this, my force will be with you," then it would have been altogether different; there's a world of difference.

I shall tell you another little story. Long ago some people used to believe that a perforated coin... It was in the days when coins were not perforated... now we have perforated coins, don't we, some countries have perforated coins, but in those days they were not perforated, and yet sometimes there were holes in a coin. And there was indeed a superstition like this, that when one found a perforated coin, it brought good luck. It brought you good luck and success in what you wanted to do.

There was a man working in an office whose life was rather poor and who was not very successful, and one day he found a perforated coin. He put it in his pocket and said to himself, "Now I am going to prosper!" And he was full of hope, courage, energy, because he knew: "Now that I have the coin, I am sure to succeed!" And, in fact, he went on prospering, prospering more and more. He earned more and more money, he had a better and better position, and people said, "What a wonderful man! How well he works! How he finds all the solutions to all problems!" Indeed, he became a remarkable man, and every morning when he put on his coat, he felt it – like this – to be sure that his coin was in his pocket.... He touched it, he felt that the coin was there, and he had confidence. And then, one day, he was a little curious, and said, "I am going to see my coin!" He was having his breakfast with his wife and said, "I am going to see my coin!" His wife told him, "Why do you want to see it? It's not necessary." "Yes, yes, let me see my coin." He took out the little bag in which he kept the coin, and found inside a coin which was not perforated!

"Ah," he said, "this is not my coin! What is this? Who has changed my coin?" Then his wife told him, "Look, one day there was some dust on your coat. I shook it off through the window and the coin fell out. I had forgotten that the coin was there. I ran to look for it but didn't find it. Someone had picked it up. So I thought you would be very unhappy and I put another coin there." *(Laughter)* Only, he, of course, was confident that his coin was there and that was enough.

Psychic power in existence
Manifold, imperious, irresistible in its understanding sweetness.
Hibiscus rosa-sinensis. Light Pink

It is the faith, the trust that does it, you see.... The perforated coin gives you nothing at all. You can always try. If you have the confidence, it gives you... When one has confidence...

There! now... and that's enough.

Questions and Answers 1954

FLOWERS, MOST OPEN TO DIVINE INFLUENCE ON THE PLANE OF MATTER

On the plane of Matter they are the most open to my influence – I can transmit a state of consciousness more easily to a flower than to a man: it is very receptive, though it does not know how to formulate its experience to itself because it lacks a mind. But the pure psychic consciousness is instinctive to it.

When, therefore, you offer flowers to me their condition is almost always an index to yours. There are persons who never succeed in bringing a fresh flower to me – even if the flower is fresh it becomes limp in their hands. Others, however, always bring fresh flowers and even revitalise drooping ones. If your aspiration is strong your flower-offerings will be fresh.

And if you are receptive you will be also very easily able to absorb the message I put in the flowers I give you. When I give them, I give you states of consciousness; the flowers are the mediums and it all depends on your receptivity whether they are effective or not.

Questions and Answers 1929-1931

THERE ARE STONES...
THAT CAN ACCUMULATE FORCES

(Student:) You say that perhaps stones also feel love?[1]

(Mother:) It is possible.

Can it be known?

One can feel it. There is a certain state of consciousness in which one perceives this divine Love wherever it is found, and one does not feel so great a difference between creatures as it appears physically. There is much more aspiration than one would think in things we call inanimate. Much more. There is also in stones a kind of

---

1 "Love is universal and eternal; it is always manifesting itself and always identical in its essence. And it is a Divine Force; for the distortions we see in its apparent workings belong to its instruments. Love does not manifest in human beings alone; it is everywhere. Its movement is there in plants, perhaps in the very stones; in the animals it is easy to detect its presence."

Questions and Answers 1929-1931

spontaneous sense of what is higher, more noble, more pure, and though they cannot express it in any way, they feel it, and this affects them differently.

Even in things, even in objects, even in stones, there is a strange receptivity which comes from this Presence. There are stones – if you know how to do it – that can accumulate forces. They can accumulate forces, keep them and transmit them. One can take stones (what are called precious stones) and concentrate forces into them and they keep them. And these forces irradiate slowly, very gradually. But if one knows how to do it one can accumulate such a quantity as would last, so to speak, indefinitely.

Are these forces of any use when they come out from the stones?

Certainly, yes! The stone can preserve the force almost indefinitely. There are those stones which can serve as a link; there are stones which can serve as a battery; there are stones which can hold a force for protection. That indeed is remarkable, my child. One can accumulate in a stone (particularly in amethysts) a force for protection, and the force truly protects the one who wears the stone. It is very interesting, I have experienced it. I knew someone who had a stone of this kind, charged with the power of protection, and it was wonderful when he wore it... There are stones which can be used to foretell events. Some people know how to read in these stones events which are going to happen. Stones can carry messages.

Naturally, this requires an ability on both sides: on one side, a sufficiently strong power of concentration; on the other, a power to see and read directly, without using very precise words either. Consequently, because they can serve as batteries, it means that they carry within them the source of the force itself, otherwise they wouldn't be receptive. It is a force of this kind that is at the origin of crystalisations, as in rock-crystals, for instance, which form such magnificent patterns, with such a complete harmony, and that comes from one thing alone, this Presence at the centre. Now, one doesn't see because one has no inner sensibility, but once one has the direct perception of the forces of love behind things, one sees that they are the same everywhere. Even in constructed things: one can come to understand what they say.

Anything else?

Questions and Answers 1953

✽

Mother, when flowers are brought to you, how do you give them a significance?

To the flowers? But it's in the same way, by entering into contact with the nature of the flower, its inner truth. Then one knows what it represents.

Questions and Answers 1953

Mother's Game of 'Precious Stones'

(Tara Jauhar:) To keep us [group of young girls] occupied, the Mother one day brought us a game which She Herself had made. It was the game of 'Precious Stones'. It had picture cards each representing a precious stone. The pictures were coloured by the Mother to show us the exact colour of the stones. Below each card She had Herself written the name of the stone. These cards would be distributed to the players and another set of cards with only the names of the stones were placed in the centre. Each player, in turn, picked up a card from the centre and if he had the corresponding card in his hand, he put both the cards aside. If not, he would replace the little card in the stack at the bottom. The player who finished all the cards first was the winner.

It was very important for us to win because at the end the Mother always asked who had won the maximum number of games and the winner was always rewarded with a chocolate or a little gift.

Le jeu des pierres précieuses

Perle blanche
Perle rose
Diamant (blanc)
Rubis (rouge)
Emeraude (vert)
Saphir (bleu)
Améthyste (violet)
Topaze (jaune)
Topaze brulée (brun)
Grenat (pourpre)

List of Precious Stones

The Mother loved games of skill. One day She told me that we should introduce to the children games which demanded a certain amount of skill. To demonstrate the importance of developing this faculty She asked each of us (one after the other) to lift the cover of a crystal bowl and put it back without making any sound. We all tried but it was only the Mother who replaced the cover without making the least sound.

Tara Jauhar, *Growing Up with the Mother*

The Mineral Kingdom

Mother begins the reading of the last six chapters of *The Life Divine*.

"A spiritual evolution, an evolution of consciousness in Matter in a constant developing self-formation till the form can reveal the indwelling Spirit, is then the key-note, the central significant motive of the terrestrial existence. This significance is concealed at the outset by the involution of the Spirit, the Divine Reality, in a dense material Inconscience; a veil of Inconscience, a veil of insensibility of Matter hides the universal Consciousness-Force which works within it, so that the Energy, which is the first form the Force of creation assumes in the physical universe, appears to be itself inconscient and yet does the works of a vast occult Intelligence."

Sri Aurobindo, *The Life Divine*,
"Man and the Evolution"

(Mother:) ... So, in the outer appearances as you see them, at first you find the mineral kingdom with stones, earth, minerals which to us, in our outer consciousness, appear absolutely unconscious. Yet, behind this unconsciousness there is the life of the Spirit, the consciousness of the Spirit, which is completely hidden, which is as if asleep – though that is only an appearance – and which works from within, in order gradually to transform this Matter that is completely inert in appearance, so that its organisation may lend itself more and more to the manifestation of consciousness. And he says here that at first this veil of inert Matter is so total that, to a superficial glance, it is something that has neither life nor consciousness. When you pick up a stone and look at it with your ordinary eyes and consciousness, you say, "It has no life, no consciousness." For one who knows how to see behind appearances, there is, hidden at the centre of this Matter – at the centre of *each atom* of this Matter – there is, hidden, the Supreme Divine Reality working from within, gradually, through the millennia, to change this inert Matter into something that is expressive enough to be able to reveal the Spirit within. Then you have the progression of the history of Life: how, from the stone, there suddenly appeared a rudimentary life and through successive species a sort of organisation, that is, an organic substance capable of revealing life. But between the mineral and vegetable kingdoms there are transitional elements, one doesn't know whether they belong to the mineral or already to the vegetable kingdom – when one studies this in detail one sees some strange species which belong neither here nor there which are not quite this and yet not quite that. Then comes the development of the vegetable kingdom where naturally life appears, for there is growth, transformation – a plant sprouts up, develops, grows – and with the first phenomenon of life comes also the phenomenon of decomposition and disintegration which is relatively much more rapid than in the stone. A stone, if protected from the impact of other forces, can last apparently indefinitely, whereas the plant already follows a curve of growth, ascent and decline and decomposition – but this with an extremely restricted consciousness ...

Questions and Answers 1957-1958

Madame David-Neel's Jewel

You know, queer things are happening here. There are certain things that literally disappear, and then, after a few days, they reappear! *(Mother looks for her note again.)* I prefer to exhaust all material explanations before making other suppositions. But even someone like Madame David-Neel (and God knows she was a positivist in the extreme) herself told me an experience of that sort. I was explaining something to her and she replied, "I am not surprised, because the same thing happened to me..." She had a jewel (it was the time when she used to wear jewels) which she used to keep at the top of a box (inside the box, but at its top). It was a Chinese dragon, and she wanted to wear it one evening. She opened the box, the jewel wasn't there anymore (yet the box was locked inside a cupboard, and there wasn't any sign of theft). She tried, she searched for it, she couldn't find it. Then, four or five days afterwards, she opened the box again, and there was the jewel, just where it was supposed to be!

Mother's Agenda, 31st July 1964

Prayers and Meditations of the Mother

(Communication received at 5.30 in the evening after meditation.)

"As thou art contemplating me, I shall speak to thee this evening. I see in thy heart a diamond surrounded by a golden light. It is at once pure and warm, something which may manifest impersonal love; but why dost thou keep this treasure enclosed in that dark casket lined with deep purple? The outermost covering is of a deep lustreless blue, a real mantle of darkness. It would seem that thou art afraid of showing thy splendour.

Learn to radiate and do not fear the storm: the wind carries us far from the shore but shows us over the world. Wouldst thou be thrifty of thy tenderness? But the source of love is infinite. Dost thou fear to be misunderstood? But where hast thou seen man capable of understanding the Divine? And if the eternal truth finds in thee a means of manifesting itself, what dost thou care for all the rest? Thou art like a pilgrim coming out of the sanctuary; standing on the threshold in front of the crowd, he hesitates before revealing his precious secret, that of his supreme discovery. Listen,

I too hesitated for days, for I could foresee both my preaching and its results: the imperfection of expression and the still greater imperfection of understanding. And yet I turned to the earth and men and brought them my message. Turn to the earth and men — isn't this the command thou always hearest in thy heart? — in thy heart, for it is that which carries a blessed message for those who are athirst for compassion. Henceforth nothing can attack the diamond. It is unassailable in its perfect constitution and the soft radiance that flashes from it can change many things in the hearts of men. Thou doubtest thy power and fearest thy ignorance? It is precisely this that wraps up thy strength in that dark mantle of starless night. Thou hesitatest and tremblest as on the threshold of a mystery, for now the mystery of the manifestation seems to thee more terrible and unfathomable than that of the Eternal Cause. But thou must take courage again and obey the injunction from the depths.

It is I who am telling thee this, for I know thee and love thee as thou didst know and love me once. I have appeared clearly before thy sight so that thou mayst in no way doubt my word. And also to thy eyes I have shown thy heart so that thou canst thus see what the supreme Truth has willed for it, so that thou mayst discover in it the law of thy being. The thing still seems to thee quite difficult: a day will come when thou wilt wonder how for so long it could have been otherwise."

— Sākyamuni, *20th December 1916*

Prayers and Meditations of the Mother

A few minutes passed in silence before Thee are worth centuries of felicity....

Grant, O Lord, that all shadows may be dispelled and that I may be more and more Thy faithful servant in constancy and serenity. Before Thee may my heart be pure as a pure crystal, so that wholly it may reflect Thee.

Oh! the sweetness of abiding in silence before Thee....

22nd November 1913

A Vision

On 28th May 1958, the Mother recounted a vision she once had of a wonderful Being of Love and Consciousness, emanated from the Supreme Origin and projected directly into the Inconscient so that the creation would gradually awaken to the Supramental Consciousness. The Mother's account of this vision was brought out in November 1906 in the Revue Cosmique, a monthly review published in Paris.

I slept and now I am awake.

I slept upon the western waters, and now I enter the ocean in order to explore its depths. Its surface is green as beryl, tinted silver by the moonlight. Beneath, the water is sapphire-blue and soon becomes faintly luminous.

I lay down upon undulations that shimmered like the ripples in moire, and now I descend, rocked from one undulation to the next by a gentle regular motion, borne straight towards the west.

As I glide downwards, the water grows more luminous and is streaked with wide silvery currents.

Thus I go on descending for a long time, rocked from undulation to undulation, down and ever further down.

Suddenly, looking upward, I notice a gleam of pink; I draw nearer and see a coral-like shrub, as large as a tree, clinging to a blue rock. Water creatures come and go in countless variety. Now I stand on the fine bright sand. I look around me in wonder. There are mountains and valleys, fantastic forests, strange flowers which could almost be animals, fish one could take for flowers – there is no separation, no interval between stationary and moving beings. Everywhere are colours, soft or vivid and iridescent, yet always refined and in harmony with one another. I walk on golden sand and gaze at all this beauty, which is bathed in a faint pale-blue radiance dotted with tiny circling spheres, red or green or golden.

How marvellous are the depths of the sea! Everywhere one feels the presence of the One in whom all harmonies dwell! I continue westwards, with no fatigue or lessening of speed. Scene follows scene in incredible variety; there, on a rock of lapis-lazuli, are fine and delicate seaweeds, like long blond or violet hair; here are great rose-coloured walls, all spangled with silver; there are flowers which seem carved from enormous diamonds; and here are goblets as fine as if they had been wrought by the most skilful of craftsmen, containing what look like drops of emerald throbbing with alternate pulsations of shadow and light.

Now I have entered on a path of silver sand between two walls of rock as blue as sapphire; the water becomes more clear and luminous.

Suddenly, at a turn in the path, I find myself before a cave which appears to be made of wrought crystal, all sparkling with rainbow light.

Between two iridescent columns stands a tall being; his face is that of a very young man, and is framed with short fair curls; his eyes are as green as the sea. He wears a light-blue tunic, and on his shoulders are great snow-white fins in place of wings. On seeing me, he stands back against a column to let me pass. Hardly have I crossed the threshold when an exquisite melody strikes my ears. Here the water is all iridescent, the ground is strewn with nacreous pearls; the entrance and the vault, from which graceful stalactites are hanging, are like opal, and delectable perfumes fill the air. Galleries, nooks and recesses open on every side, but straight in front of me I see a great light, and towards that I direct my steps. This light is made of wide rays of gold, silver, sapphire and emerald and ruby, all issuing from a point too distant for me to distinguish what it is, and streaming out in all directions. I feel myself being drawn towards their centre by a powerful attraction.

Now I can see the source of these rays and I behold an oval of white light, haloed by a splendid rainbow. The oval is lying horizontally, and I sense that the one whom the light hides from my view is deep in sleep. I stand long at the outer edge of the rainbow, peering through the light to see the one who lies sleeping in such splendour. Unable to distinguish anything in this way, I enter first the rainbow, and then the shining white oval. Now I see a marvellous being, lying on what seems to be a mass of white down; his lithe, incomparably beautiful body is clothed in a long white robe. Of his head, which rests on his folded arm, I can see only his long locks, the colour of ripe grain, flowing down over his shoulders. A powerful and sweet emotion floods through me at this magnificent sight, and also a profound reverence.

Has the sleeper sensed my presence? Now he awakes, and rises in all his grace and beauty. He turns towards me and his eyes meet mine, eyes that are mauve and shining, full of infinite sweetness and tenderness. Without a word, he bids me a loving welcome, to which my whole being joyously responds; then, taking me by the hand, he leads me to the couch he has just left. I lie down upon this downy whiteness and the harmonious visage leans over me. A sweet flow of force suffuses me entirely, vitalising, revivifying each cell.

Then, surrounded by the splendid rainbow hues, wrapped in soothing melodies and exquisite perfumes, beneath that powerful and tender gaze I fell asleep in a beatific repose. And in my sleep I learned many beautiful and useful things.

Of all the marvellous things that I understood without the sound of words, I shall mention only one.

Wherever there is beauty, wherever there is radiance, wherever there is progress towards perfection, be it in the Heavens of the heights or in the Heavens of the depths, there, surely, beings will be found in the form and likeness of man – man, the supreme agent of terrestrial evolution.

The Mother

The Mother's Diamond Light

The diamond is the symbol of the Mother's light and energy – the diamond light is that of her consciousness at its most intense.

*

1. It [the diamond light] means essential Force of the Mother.
2. The diamond light proceeds from the heart of the Divine Consciousness and it brings the opening of the Divine Consciousness wherever it goes.
3. The Mother's diamond light is a light of absolute purity and power.
4. The diamond light is the central consciousness and force of the Divine.

*

The diamond is the symbol of the intensest light of the Mother's consciousness, so your visions indicate that you saw her full of that light and radiating it. Other jewels must be symbols of other forces, the Ruby indicating power in the physical.

Sri Aurobindo, *Letters on The Mother*

Sri Aurobindo is wearing on his left index finger a golden ring with Mother's symbol and a diamond in the centre.

Earth with its seven Jewel - Centres

Sri Aurobindo

Seven times seven are the planes of the Supreme Goddess, the steps of ascent and descent of the Divine Transcendent and Universal Adyashakti.

Above are the thrice seven supreme planes of Sat-Chit-Ananda; in between are the seven planes of the Divine Truth and Vastness, Mahad Brahma; below are the thrice seven steps of the ascent and descent into this evolutionary world of the earth existence.

These three gradations are successively Supermind or Truth-Mind, with its seven Suns; Life with its seven Lotuses; Earth with its seven Jewel-Centres.

The seven Lotuses are the seven cakras of the Tantric tradition, descending and ascending from Mind (Sahasradala, Ajna, Visuddha, Anahata) that take up Life through Life in Force (Manipura, Swadhisthana) down to Life involved in Matter (Muladhara).

All these Life-Centres are in themselves centres of Truth in Life even as the seven Suns are each a flaming heart of Truth in luminous Divine-Mind-Existence; but these lotuses have been veiled, closed, shut into their own occult energies by the Ignorance. Hence the obscurity, falsehood, death, suffering of our existence.

The Jewel-Centres of the Earth Mother are seven luminous jewel-hearts of Truth in Substance; but they have been imprisoned in darkness, fossilised in immobility, veiled, closed, shut into their own occult energies by the hardness, darkness and inertia of the material Inconscience.

To liberate all these powers by the luminous and flaming descent of the Suns of the Supermind and the release of the eighth Sun of Truth hidden in the Earth, in the darkness of the Inconscience, in the cavern of Vala and his Panis, this is the first step towards the restoration of the Earth Mother to her own divinity and the earth-existence to its native light, truth, life and bliss of immaculate Ananda.

The Hour of God

The Stone Goddess

In a town of gods, housed in a little shrine,
    From sculptured limbs the Godhead looked at me, –
A living Presence deathless and divine,
    A Form that harboured all infinity.

The great World-Mother and her mighty will
    Inhabited the earth's abysmal sleep,
Voiceless, omnipotent, inscrutable,
    Mute in the desert and the sky and deep.

Now veiled with mind she dwells and speaks no word,
    Voiceless, inscrutable, omniscient,
Hiding until our soul has seen, has heard
    The secret of her strange embodiment,

One in the worshipper and the immobile shape,
A beauty and mystery flesh or stone can drape.

                          Sri Aurobindo

In tapestried chambers and on crystal floors
Excerpts from Sri Aurobindo's *Savitri – A Legend and A Symbol*

The inner planes uncovered their **crystal doors**;
Strange powers and influences touched his life.

p.28

In a brief moment caught, a little space,
All-Knowledge packed into great wordless thoughts
Lodged in the expectant stillness of his depths
A **crystal** of the ultimate Absolute,
A portion of the inexpressible Truth
Revealed by silence to the silent soul.

p.38

A graph shall be of many meeting worlds,
A cube and **union-crystal** of the gods;
A Mind shall think behind Nature's mindless mask,
A conscious Vast fill the old dumb brute Space.

p.100

In the impalpable field of secret self,
This little outer being's vast support
Parted from vision by earth's solid fence,
He came into a magic **crystal air**
And found a life that lived not by the flesh,
A light that made visible immaterial things.

                                                           p.103

As if a beckoning finger of secrecy
Outstretched into a **crystal** mood of air,
Pointing at him from some near hidden depth...

                                                           p.289

Out of those **crystal windows** gleamed a will
That brought a large significance to life.

                                                           p.357

All beautiful things eternal seem and new
To virgin wonder in her **crystal soul**.

                                                           p.422

Far now behind lay Madra's spacious halls,
The white carved pillars, the cool dim alcoves,
The tinged mosaic of the **crystal floors**,
The towered pavilions, the wind-rippled pools
And gardens humming with the murmur of bees,
Forgotten soon or a pale memory
The fountain's plash in the white stone-bound pool...

                                                           p.466

Here, living centre of that vision of peace,
A Woman sat in clear and **crystal light**:
Heaven had unveiled its lustre in her eyes,
Her feet were moonbeams, her face was a bright sun...

                                                                     p.514

But mid the thinking high-built lives of men
In tapestried chambers and on crystal floors,
In armoured town or gardened pleasure-walks...

                                                                      p.533

Addict of the roseate luxury of thy thoughts,
Turn not thy gaze within thyself to look
At visions in the gleaming **crystal**, Mind,
Close not thy lids to dream the forms of Gods.

                                                                      p.616

Great forms of deities sat in deathless tiers,
Eyes of an unborn gaze towards her leaned
Through a transparency of **crystal fire**.

                                                                      p.676

And make thee a vivid knot of all my bliss
And build in thee my proud and **crystal home**.
Thy days shall be my shafts of power and light...

                                                                      p.698

The Making of the Matrimandir Crystal Globe

The crystal for the Matrimandir arrived in Auroville on 26th April 1991 at 10.15 p.m. It was moved into the Matrimandir's Inner Chamber the very next day at 9.45 a.m.

The size of 70 cm diameter was marked on the original plan that Mother had drawn for the central object in the Chamber. In July 1983, the searchlight fell on the firm of Schott in Mainz, and somewhat later on Zeiss in Oberkochen, both in Germany. These firms proposed the type of crystal – optically perfect glass – with the name of Bohr Kron 7. On the 8th June 1984, Zeiss presented the study, and gave the estimate: approx. 230,000 German Marks.

On 12th May 1987, Schott wrote to Zeiss that the cast has been done, and that the mould was being cooled. When two months later a visit to Zeiss was made, it appeared that this casting was the second one, the first one having failed for unpublished reasons.

The casting at Schott's in Mainz lasted 15 hours, and was done in a special form of refractory stone, held together by seven metal bands, which was placed on top of a platform built of iron and steel. During the casting process the glass in the form was kept at a constant temperature. After 15 hours the rough casting in the form of a massive dome with a diameter of 80 to 85 cm and a weight of 1,100 kg was finished, after which it was cooled down extremely slowly (to avoid tension) in an annealing furnace for a period of 5 weeks. The rough form had to be polished on two sides, in order to test the quality of the glass.

Finally, at the beginning of 1991, it became clear that the process to deliver the Globe could be started.

On 26th April 1991 the crystal came to the Matrimandir

The Inner Chamber of the Matrimandir was ready to receive the Crystal Globe, which at the time was the biggest ever made in the world. After casting by Schott, it was polished and finished by the Zeiss Company of West Germany. Made of pure crystal-clear glass one could see numerous reflections in it, yet the crystal retained its own individuality and splendour.

(Huta:) On 26th April 1991 it came to the Matrimandir at 10 o'clock at night from abroad.

In August I was invited by Piero and Gloria to have a glimpse of it. I found the crystal globe incredible.

Piero was very happy, because of the completion – the last magnificent image to be installed in the middle of the Inner Chamber, which was the Mother's Vision.

On 22nd August 1991 this wonderful crystal globe was placed in the middle of the Inner Chamber. It rested on the model of Sri Aurobindo's symbol; later the crystal globe was installed on Sri Aurobindo's symbol made out of pure gold.

(gold-plated stainless steel)

Arrival of the crystal globe in the Matriandir Chamber, 27th April 1991

Prayers and Meditations of the Mother

O Divine Master of love and purity, grant that in its stages, its smallest activities, this instrument which wants to serve Thee worthily may be purified of all egoism, all error, all obscurity, so that nothing in it may impair, deform or stop Thy action. How many little recesses lie yet in shadow, far from the full light of Thy illumination: for these I ask the supreme happiness of this illumination.

Oh, to be the pure flawless crystal which lets Thy divine ray pass without obscuring, colouring, or distorting it! — not from a desire for perfection but so that Thy work may be done as perfectly as possible.

And when I ask Thee this, the 'I' which speaks to Thee is the entire Earth, aspiring to be this pure diamond, a perfect reflector of Thy supreme light. All the hearts of men beat within my heart, all their thoughts vibrate in my thought, the slightest aspiration of a docile animal or a modest plant unite with my formidable aspiration, and all this rises towards Thee, for the conquest of Thy love and light, scaling the summits of Being to attain Thee, ravish Thee from Thy motionless beatitude and make Thee penetrate the darkness of suffering to transform it into divine Joy, into sovereign Peace. And this violence is made of an infinite love which gives itself and trustful security which smiles with the certitude of Thy perfect Unity.

O my sweet Master, Thou art the Triumpher and the Triumph, the Victor and the Victory!

25th May 1914

The Crystal of the Matrimandir

(Satprem:) Sweet Mother, I have told Paolo [an Italian disciple, a designer] to come, he is waiting outside.

Yes. There is an interesting thing. For a long time I had been feeling something, then we spoke about it the other day and I *saw* it. I spoke of it to Roger [Auroville's architect], I told him to see Paolo and I also told him that I had *seen* what should be done. Of course he did not say No, he said Yes to everything, but I felt that he did not really intend... But, this is what happened. I saw clearly–very, very distinctly.... That is to say it was like that and it is still like that, it is there (*gesture indicating an eternal plane*)... the interior of this place....

It will be a kind of hall like the inside of a column. No windows. The ventilation will be artificial, with those machines (*gesture indicating an air-conditioner*) and only a roof. And the sun striking the centre. Or when there is no sun – at night and on cloudy days – an electric spotlight.

And the idea is to build right now a sort of example or model to hold about a hundred people. When the town is built and we have had the experience, we will make it into something big. But then it will be very big, to hold a thousand to two thousand people. And the second one will be built around the first: that means, the first one will not go until the second one is finished. That is the idea.

Only, so as to talk about it to Paolo (and if possible, if I see that it is possible, to talk about it to Roger), I wanted to have a plan. I will have it made, not myself, because I can't any more; I would have been able to do it at one time, but now I don't see well enough. I will have it done this afternoon, in front of me, a plan, and with this plan I will be able to explain really well. But to you I simply wanted to say what I have seen.

It will be a tower with twelve facets, each facet represents a month of the year; and up above, the roof of the tower will be like this (*gesture indicating a roof which slopes upwards from the sides to the centre*).

And then, inside, there will be twelve columns. The walls and then twelve columns. And right at the centre, on the floor, there is my symbol, and above it four of Sri Aurobindo's symbols, joined to form a square, and above that... a globe. If possible, a globe made of transparent material, and with or without light inside, but the sun should strike the globe; then according to the month, the time, it will be from here, from there, from there (*gesture indicating the movement of the sun*). You understand? There will always be an opening with a ray. Not a diffused light: a ray which strikes, which should strike. It will require some technical knowledge to be able to carry it out, and that is why I want to make a design with an engineer.

And then, there will be no windows or lights inside. It will always be in a kind of clear half-light, day and night – by day with the sun, by night with artificial light. And on the floor, nothing, just a floor like this one (*in Mother's room*). That is to say, first wood (wood or something else), then a sort of rubber foam, thick, very soft, and then a carpet. A carpet everywhere, everywhere except at the centre. And people will be able to sit everywhere. And the twelve columns are for people who need support for their backs!

And then, people will not come for a regular meditation or anything of that kind (but the inner organisation will be made afterwards): it will be a place for concentration. Not everyone will be able to come; there will be a time in the week or a time in the day (I don't know) when visitors will be allowed to come, but anyway, no mixture. A fixed time or a fixed day for showing people around, and the rest of time only for those who are… serious – serious, sincere, who want to learn to concentrate.

So I think that is good. It was there (*gesture upward*). I still see it when I speak of it – I *see*. As I see it, it is very beautiful, it is really very beautiful… a sort of half-light: one can see, but it is *very* tranquil. And then, very clear and very bright rays of light (the spotlight, the

artificial light, must be rather golden, it must not be cold – that will depend on the spotlight) onto the symbol. A globe made of a plastic material or… I don't know.

Crystal?

If it is possible, yes. For the small temple the globe will not need to be very big: if it were as big as this (*about thirty centimetres*) it would be good. But for the big temple it will have to be big.

But how will the big temple be built? On top of the small one?

No, no, the small one will go. But the big one will be built later, and on a vast scale… the small one will go only after the big one is built. But of course, for the town to be finished, it will take about twenty years (for everything to be really in order, in its place). It is like the gardens: all the gardens which are being made are for now, but in twenty years all that will have to be on another scale; then, it must be something really… really beautiful.

And I wonder what material should be used to make this globe, the big one?… The small one, in crystal perhaps: a globe like that (*thirty centimetres*). I think that will be enough. One must be able to see the globe from every corner of the room.

It shouldn't be raised too high above the floor either?

No, Sri Aurobindo's symbol does not need to be big. It should be so big (*gesture*)...

Twenty-five, thirty centimetres?

At the most, at the very most.

That means that it will be at about eye-level?

Eye-level, yes, that's it.
And a *very* tranquil atmosphere. And *nothing*, you see – great columns... It remains to be seen whether the style of the columns should be... whether they will be round, or if they will also have twelve facets.... And *twelve* columns.

And a roof in two sections?

Yes, a roof in two sections so as to have the sun. It must be arranged in such a way that the rain cannot come in. We cannot think of having to open and close something when it rains, it is not possible. It must be arranged in such a way that the rain cannot get in. But the sun must enter as rays, not diffused. So the opening must be small. It needs an engineer who really knows his job.

And when would they start?

I would like to begin at once, as soon as we have the plans. Only, there are two questions: first the plans (we can get the workers) and then the money…. I think that it is possible with this idea of making a sort of small model (of course "small" is a manner of speaking, because to be able to hold a hundred people easily it still needs to be quite big), a small model to begin with, and then while making the small model they will learn, and the big one will be made only when the town is finished – not right now.

I spoke about it to Roger, who told me the next day: "Yes, but it will take time to prepare." I didn't say anything about all that I've just told you, I only spoke of doing something. And afterwards I had the vision of this room – so I no longer need anyone to see what it should be: I know. And it requires an engineer rather than an architect, because an architect… it must be as simple as possible.

I told Paolo what you had seen, this great empty room; it moved him very much. This great empty room was just what he saw. He understands quite well. Well, empty – that means simply a form.

But a form… Like a tower, but… (that's why I wanted to have a sketch, to show it) twelve regular facets, and then there should be a wall, not an upright wall but something like this (*slightly inclined gesture*). I don't know if it is possible. And inside, twelve columns. And then an arrangement must be found to catch the sun. Twelve facets in such a way that at any time of the year it can come. It needs someone who knows the job well.

The outside... I did not see the outside, I did not see it at all. I saw only the inside.

I wanted to explain to Paolo when I had the papers. It would be easier, but since you have called him...

(Sujata goes and brings Paolo to the room. Mother tells him:)

After we decided to build this temple, I saw it, I saw it from the inside. I have just tried to describe it to Satprem. But in a few days I will have some plans and drawings, so I will be able to explain more clearly. Because I don't know at all how it is outside, but inside I know.

(Paolo:) The outside grows from the inside.

It is a kind of tower with twelve regular facets, which represent the twelve months of the year, and it is absolutely empty.... And it must be able to hold from a hundred to two hundred people. And then, to support the roof there will be twelve columns inside (not outside), and right at the centre, well, the object of concentration.... And with the collaboration of the sun, all the year round the sun should enter as rays: no diffusion, an arrangement must be made so that it can enter as rays. Then according to the time of day and the month of the year, the ray will turn (there will be an arrangement up above) and the ray will be directed onto the centre. At the centre there will be the symbol of Sri Aurobindo, supporting a globe. A globe which we shall try to make from something transparent like crystal or... A big globe. And then, people will be allowed in to concentrate – (*Mother laughs*) to learn to concentrate! No fixed meditations, none of all that, but they must stay there in silence, in silence and concentration.

(Paolo:) It is very beautiful.

But the place is absolutely... as simple as possible. And the floor in such a way that people are comfortable, so that they don't have to think that it hurts them here or it hurts them there!

(Paolo:) It is very beautiful.

And in the middle, on the floor, my symbol. At the centre of my symbol we will put, in four parts, like a square, four symbols of Sri Aurobindo, upright, supporting a transparent globe. That has been seen.

So I am going to have some small plans prepared by an engineer, simple ones, to show, and then I will show you when it is ready. So. And then we will see. The walls will probably have to be of concrete.

(Paolo:) The whole structure can be in reinforced concrete.

The roof should probably be sloping, and then at the centre there will have to be a special arrangement for the sun.

(Satprem:) You said that the walls would be slightly sloping.

Either the walls or the roof should be sloping – whichever is the easiest to do. The walls could be made straight and the roof sloping. And the upper part of the roof resting on the twelve columns, and up above, the arrangement for the sun.

And inside, nothing; nothing but the columns. The columns, I don't know, we will have to see whether they should be made with facets (like the roof, with twelve facets) or else simply round.

(Paolo:) Round.

Or simply square – it remains to be seen.
And then, on the floor, we will put something thick and soft. Here – you are comfortable as you are sitting? Yes? First there is wood, and then this kind of rubber, and on top of it a woollen carpet.

(Satprem:) With your symbol?

Not the carpet. For the symbol, I had thought it would be better to make it out of something durable.

(Paolo:) It should be in stone.

The symbol… everything will be around it, of course. The symbol will not cover it all, it will be only in the middle of the space – (*Mother laughs*) they mustn't sit on the symbol! – that, in the middle.

The proportion of the symbol to the whole will have to be considered very carefully in relation to the height.

(Paolo:) And the room quite large?

Oh yes, it has to be... it should be like a sort of half-light with these rays of sunlight, so that the ray can be *seen*. A ray of sunlight. Then according to the time of day, the sun will turn (with the time of day and the month of the year). And then at night, as soon as the sun disappears, spotlights are lit which will have the same effect and the same colour. And day and night the light remains there. But no windows or lamps or anything like that – nothing. Ventilation with air-conditioners (they are built into the walls, it is very easy). And silence. Inside no one speaks! (*Mother laughs*) That will be good. So, as soon as my papers are ready, I will call you and show them to you.

(Paolo:) Very good.
(Paolo leaves. Mother then continues speaking with Satprem.)

I did not ask Paolo if he had seen Roger because... Roger is completely in the "practical" atmosphere of today. It is good – it must get started!

You see, this is what I have learned: the failure of the religions. It is because they were divided. They wanted people to be religious to the exclusion of the other religions; and every branch of knowledge has been a failure because they were exclusive; and man has been a failure because he was exclusive. And what the new consciousness wants (it is on this that it insists) is: no more divisions. To be able to understand the spiritual extreme, the material extreme, and to find... to find the meeting-point, the point where... that becomes a real force.

From the practical point of view I will try to make Roger understand; but I have seen, it seemed to me that what is needed... Roger, when he is here, looks after Auromodèle, the practical side, all that. It is very necessary, it is very good; and for the building of the Centre, I would like Paolo to do it, and so I would like Paolo to stay when Roger is away; Paolo should be here when Roger is gone, and we shall do it with Paolo. Only I don't want either of them to feel that it is one of them against the other. They must understand that it is to complement one another. I think Paolo will understand.

But Roger might take that as an encroachment on his responsibilities?

Perhaps not. I will try, I will try.

No, when I told him that it was necessary to build the Centre, that I had seen it and that it should be done, he did not object. He only told me, "But it will take time." I told him, "No, it must be done at once." And that is why I am having these sketches made by an engineer to show to him, because it is not an architect's job, it is an engineer's job, with very precise calculations for the light of the sun, very precise. It needs someone who really knows. The architect has to see that the columns are beautiful, that the walls are beautiful, that the proportions are correct – all that is very good – and then the symbol at the centre. The aspect of beauty, of course the architect should see to that, but the whole calculation aspect… And the important thing is this, the play of the sun onto the centre. Because that becomes the symbol – the symbol of the future realisation.

Area below the Matrimandir

Below the Matrimandir, the architect initially wanted to create a lotus pond, but when he realised that lotuses will not bloom in the shade, instead of plants he used 216 petal-shaped marble slabs to create a pond over which water flows from the outside towards the centre. Now this feature itself is known as "the Lotus Pond".

At the centre of this pond, there is a natural crystal globe (17cm dia.) which receives the beam of sunlight which permeates Matrimandir from top to bottom, as if to illumine the depths. A symbol of the Mother clad in white marble allows the sunbeam to pass through its central point at the base of the Matrimandir sphere and fall onto the small crystal globe.

Sitting areas for concentration have been created within the pillars named for the Mother's four *Aspects* or *Personalities*: Maheshwari, Mahakali, Mahalakshmi, Mhasaraswati.

Matrimandir, the Soul of Auroville

Literally in Sanskrit 'Temple of the Mother' (though it is not in fact a temple), the Matrimandir is seen as the "Soul of Auroville".

It is a huge gold-disc-clad structure in the form of a slightly flattened globe akin to a tantric *shalagrama*, or primal egg of Brahman, representing the unity of creation. Measuring 36m in diameter by 29m in height, it sits on four double support pillars facing North, East, South and West representing the four aspects, or personalities, of the Divine Mother: Mahakali to the north for her Strength, Mahalakshmi to the east for her Beauty and Harmony, Maheshwari to the south for her Wisdom, and Mahasaraswati to the west for her Perfection.

The outer surface of the Matrimandir is covered with more than 1,400 golden discs in two basic sizes, the small ones (approx two-thirds) up to 1.6m in diameter and the large ones (approx one-third) up to 2.4m in diameter. By "golden" one does in fact refer to real gold, because 24-carat gold leaf has been used, sealed at 800°C between thin sheets of glass in over 2.3 million 4x4 cm tiles, which are bonded onto the stainless steel discs: over 2,000 onto each of the large discs and up to 1,200 on the smaller discs.

Regarding the discs, there are two frequently asked questions. The first is what is their purpose, and the second is why gold?

The answer to the first is that the discs serve no specific purpose beyond helping to cool the inner structure by reflecting the sun's rays, i.e. their purpose is primarily aesthetic. As to the second question, why gold, the same question could be asked of the Golden Temple of the Sikhs in Amritsar, or the Sanctum Sanctorum of many of India's great temples, where one almost invariably finds gold. Why? Because it is the most precious, most beautiful and purest element we have to enshrine the Divine, or God within.

As to the siting of the Matrimandir, it is located close to the Banyan Tree, the geographical centre of Auroville, and to the Amphitheatre in the Park of Unity at the centre of the township. Its all-white marble-clad Inner Chamber – where a shaft of sunlight, or artificial light at night, focuses down onto a perfect 70 cms diameter optical-quality glass sphere (the 'Crystal') surrounded by 12 white columns – is a place for silent concentration only, free of any ceremonies, rituals, offerings, music, incense, flowers or religious forms.

Matrimandir's Inner Skin

(Satprem:) Mother, one last thing, a question asked by the person who wrote the letter: he asks whether the "vast Grace-Light" or "Truth-Light" the Swami[1] mentions is the supramental light?

Which light?

The vast "Grace-Light."

Grace-Light…. Oh, I liked that very much in his letter. Grace-Light, that's what is working, you know: the work being done through this [Mother's body] is exactly like that, it's exactly like a Grace-Light. I liked that a lot. It's exactly that.

You see, it's a light with several degrees, and in the most material it's slightly… it must be the supramental force, because it's slightly golden, slightly pinkish (you know that light), but very, very pale. One of them *(gesture pointing to another, higher layer)* is white like

---

[1] Thiruvarutprakasa Vallalār Chidambaram Ramalingam (5th October 1823 – 30th January 1874), also known as Vallalār, Ramalinga Swamigal and Ramalinga Adigal, he founded a group known as "Samarasa Suddha Sanmarga Sathiya Sangam".

milk, opaque – it's very strong. And there's another *(gesture very high)* which is white like... it's transparent light. With that one, it's strange: one drop of it on the hostile forces, and they're dissolved. They melt like this *(gesture before one's very eyes)*. I said all that to Sri Aurobindo, he completely confirmed it. That's essentially the Grace in its... *(gesture very high)* supreme state. It's a Light... it has no colour, you know, it's transparent, and that Light (I have experienced that, I mention it because I know it), if you put it on a hostile being... it melts like that. It's extraordinary.... And then, in its "benevolent" form, as we might call it (that is to say, the Grace helping and assisting and healing), it's white like milk. And if I want a wholly material action (but this is quite recent – it's since this new Consciousness came), then in its physical action, on the physical, it's become slightly coloured: it's luminous, golden with some pink in it, but it's not pink... *(Mother takes a hibiscus next to her)*. It's like this.

Like Auroville's flower?

Like Auroville's flower. But I DELIBERATELY chose it as Auroville's flower, for that reason. And my impression is that this is the supramental colour: when I see beings from the supramental, they have... not quite this colour... It's not like a flower, it's like flesh. But it's like this *(Mother points to the flower's colour)*.

Mother's Agenda, 11th July 1970

View from the second level of the Matrimandir, where the two ramps start their spiral journey up to the chamber. The appearance of the interior is one of spaciousness with the white curving line of the ramps and the second level seen against the glowing orange spherical shell of the inner skin.

The frame of the inner skin consists of aluminium triangles. During the daytime, the sun lights up the inner skin through salmon-orange coloured portholes behind the golden disks. In the evenings, Light Emitting Diodes (LEDs) of three different colours are used to obtain the required colour. A simple computerized control system allows the light in each triangle to be adjusted in intensity and colour.

The Mother's Presence and the living Action of Her Grace

On 12th May 1974, early in the morning I had a very powerful dream-vision. I saw a column of white Light descending from above, both the edges of the white Light fringed with a golden tint. The column of Light went down into a dark pit which had a round opening. The white Light gave an impression of an intensity which was at the same time sweet, calm and soothing. The descent continued for a minute or two. When it was over, the pit was filled with white Light, and there hung over it a bright haze which was very beautiful.

The dream-vision was very vivid and concrete. I informed Nolini-da about it. He answered:

Huta,

It is a true and very beautiful experience. Naturally it is Mother's Presence and the living Action of Her Grace.

Huta

Encyclopedic Overview of Crystals

A **crystal** is any solid material in which the component atoms are arranged in a definite pattern and whose surface regularity reflects its internal symmetry.

The earliest crystal grower was nature. Many excellent crystals of minerals formed in the geologic past are found in mines and caves throughout the world. Most precious and semiprecious stones are well-formed crystals. Early efforts to produce synthetic crystals were concentrated on making gems. Synthetic ruby was grown by the French scientist Marc Antoine Augustin Gaudin in 1873. Since about 1950 scientists have learned to grow in the laboratory crystals of quality equal or superior to those found in nature. New techniques for growth are continually being developed, and crystals with three or more atoms per unit cell are continually being discovered.

Gemstones

Gemstones are various minerals highly prized for beauty, durability, and rarity. A few noncrystalline materials of organic origin (e.g., pearl, red coral, and amber) also are classified as gemstones.

Gemstones have attracted humankind since ancient times, and have long been used for jewelry. The prime requisite for a gem is that it must be beautiful. The beauty may lie in colour or lack of colour; in the latter case, extreme limpidity and "fire" may provide the attraction. Iridescence, opalescence, asterism (the exhibition of a star-shaped figure in reflected light), chatoyance (the exhibition of a changeable lustre and a narrow, undulating band of white light), pattern, and lustre are other features that may make a gemstone beautiful. A gem must also be durable, if the stone is to retain the polish applied to it and withstand the wear and tear of constant handling.

In addition to their use as jewelry, gems were regarded by many civilizations as miraculous and endowed with mysterious powers. Different stones were endowed with different and sometimes overlapping attributes; the diamond, for instance, was thought to give its wearer strength in battle and to protect him against ghosts and magic. Vestiges of such beliefs persist in the modern practice of wearing a birthstone.

Of the more than 2,000 identified natural minerals, fewer than 100 are used as gemstones and only 16 have achieved importance. These are beryl, chrysoberyl, corundum, diamond, feldspar, garnet, jade, lazurite, olivine, opal, quartz, spinel, topaz, tourmaline, turquoise, and zircon. Some of these minerals provide more than one type of gem; beryl, for example, provides emeralds and aquamarines, while corundum provides rubies and sapphires.

Of decisive significance for the modern treatment of gemstones was the kind of cutting known as faceting, which produces brilliance by the refraction and reflection of light. Until the late Middle Ages, gems of all kinds were simply cut either en cabochon (i.e., with a rounded upper surface and a flat underside) or, especially for purposes of incrustation, into flat platelets. The rose cut was developed in the 17th century, and the brilliant cut, now the general favourite for diamonds, is said to have been used for the first time about 1700.

Quartz

Quartz is a widely distributed mineral of many varieties that consists primarily of silica, or silicon dioxide (SiO_2). Minor impurities such as lithium, sodium, potassium, and titanium may be present. Quartz has attracted attention from the earliest times; water-clear crystals were known to the ancient Greeks as *krystallos*—hence the name *crystal*, or more commonly *rock crystal*, applied to this variety. The name *quartz* is an old German word of uncertain origin first used by Georgius Agricola in 1530.

Many varieties of quartz are gemstones, including amethyst, citrine, smoky quartz, and rose quartz.

Quartz is piezoelectric: a crystal develops positive and negative charges on alternate prism edges when it is subjected to pressure or tension. The charges are proportional to the change in pressure. Because of its piezoelectric property, a quartz plate can be used as a pressure gauge, as in depth-sounding apparatus. The converse effect is that alternating opposite charges will cause alternating expansion and contraction. A section cut from a quartz crystal with definite orientation and dimensions has a natural frequency of this expansion and contraction (i.e., vibration) that is very high, measured in millions of vibrations per second.

Properly cut plates of quartz are used for frequency control in radios, televisions, and other electronic communications equipment and for crystal-controlled clocks and watches.

Electron

The electron on which forms and worlds are built,
Leaped into being, a particle of God.
A spark from the eternal Energy spilt,
It is the Infinite's blind minute abode.

In that small flaming chariot Shiva rides.
The One devised innumerably to be;
His oneness in invisible forms he hides,
Time's tiny temples to eternity.

Atom and molecule in their unseen plan
Buttress an edifice of strange onenesses,
Crystal and plant, insect and beast and man, —
Man on whom the World-Unity shall seize,

Widening his soul-spark to an epiphany
Of the timeless vastness of Infinity.

Sri Aurobindo

References

CWSA = The Complete Works of Sri Aurobindo
MCW = Collected Works of the Mother

p.12	CWSA–32, *The Mother with Letters on the Mother*, "The Mother's Symbol"
p.14-26	CWSA–30, *Letters on Yoga – III*, "Lights and Colours"
p.15 (Sincerity)	MCW–8, *Questions and Answers 1956*
p.16 (Humility)	*Mother's Agenda*, 21 December 1957
p.17 (Gratitude)	MCW–15, *Words of the Mother – III*, "Messages for Sri Aurobindo's Arrival in Pondicherry"
	Mother's Agenda, 21 December 1963
p.18 (Perseverance)	MCW–7, *Questions and Answers 1955*
	MCW–8, *Questions and Answers 1956*
p.19 (Aspiration)	MCW–5, *Questions and Answers 1953*
p.20 (Receptivity)	MCW–14, *Words of the Mother – II*, "Openness and Receptivity"
p.21 (Progress)	MCW–8, *Questions and Answers 1956*
p.22 (Courage)	MCW–15, *Words of the Mother – III*, "Messages for the Mother's First Arrival in Pondicherry"

p.23 (Goodness)	MCW–3, *Questions and Answers 1929-1931*
p.24 (Generosity)	MCW–3, *Questions and Answers 1929-1931*
p.25 (Equality)	*Mother's Agenda*, 25 February 1961
p.26 (Peace)	MCW–8, *Questions and Answers 1957-1958* MCW–15, *Words of the Mother – III*, "Illness and Health"
pp.30-39	CWSA–30, *Letters on Yoga – III*, "Lights and Colours"
pp.44-49	Huta, *The Spirit of Auroville*, Havyāvahana Trust, Pondicherry, 2002
pp.51-53	MCW–8, *Questions and Answers 1957-1958*
pp.54-55	MCW–4, *Questions and Answers 1950-1951*
pp.57-69	MCW–6, *Questions and Answers 1954* MCW–3, *Questions and Answers 1929-1931*
pp.70-73	MCW–5, *Questions and Answers 1953*
pp.74-75	Tara Jauhar, *Growing Up With The Mother*, Third Edition 2015, published by Sri Aurobindo Ashram – Delhi Branch Trust for Sri Aurobindo Education Society, New Delhi
pp.76-79	MCW–8, *Questions and Answers 1957-1958*
p.80	*Mother's Agenda*, 31 July 1964
pp.81-83	MCW–1, *Prayers and Meditations*
pp.85-89	*Mother India: Monthly Review of Culture*, Vol. LXIII, No. 12

p.91	CWSA–32, *The Mother with Letters on the Mother*, "The Mother's Lights"
pp.93-94	Sri Aurobindo, *The Hour of God*, "The Seven Centres of the Life", First edition 1959 CWSA–11, *Record of Yoga – II*, "Undated Notes, c. December 1926"
p.96	CWSA–2, *Collected Poems*
pp.98-102	CWSA–33-34, *Savitri – A Legend and A Symbol*
pp.104-105	Auroville website, "Matrimandir – Technical Information", accessed 2024
pp.106-107	Huta, *The Spirit of Auroville*, Havyāvahana Trust, Pondicherry, 2002
pp.108-109	MCW–1, *Prayers and Meditations*
pp.111-124	MCW–13, *Words of the Mother – I*, "Matrimandir Talks", 3 January 1970
pp.130-132	*Mother's Agenda*, 11 July 1970
p.134	Huta, *The Spirit of Auroville*, Havyāvahana Trust, Pondicherry, 2002
pp.136-139	Encyclopaedia Britannica online, "Crystals (physics)", "Quartz (mineral)", "Gemstone (mineral)", accessed 2024
p.140	CWSA–2, *Collected Poems*

Further Resources

Books:

Edgar Cayce Guide to Gemstones, Minerals, Metals and More
by Shelley Kaehr, Ph.D.,
2005, A.R.E. Press, Virginia Beach, Virginia, USA

Edgar Cayce on the power of Color, Stones and Crystals
by Dan Campbell under the editorship of Charles Thomas Cayce,
1989, Grand Central Publishing, New York, Boston

Edgar Cayce on Prophecy
by Mary Ellen Carter under the editorship of Hugh Lynn Cayce,
1968, Warner Books Edition, New York

Love is in the Earth: A Kaleidoscope of Crystals by Melody,
1993, Earth Love Publishing House, Colorado 80033, USA

Stone Medicine: A Chinese Medical Guide to Healing with Gems and Minerals by Leslie J. Franks,
2016, Healing Arts Press, Rochester, Vermont, Toronto, Canada

The Crystal Bible by Judy Hall,
2009, A Godsfield Book, UK

Videos available on YouTube:

Vogel Cut Crystals Complete Documentary by Ross Newkirk (53:01)

Activating your Spiritual Potential through Angels, Crystals, Colors and Metals w/ Dr. Robert Gilbert,
Aubrey Marcus Podcast, 2024 (2:42:02)

International Publications

Auroville Architecture
by Franz Fassbender

Auroville Form Style and Design
by Franz Fassbender

Landscapes and Gardens of Auroville
by Franz Fassbender

Inauguration of Auroville
by Franz Fassbender

Auroville in a Nutshell
by Tim Wrey

Death doesn't exist
The Mother on Death, Sri Aurobindo on Rebirth
Compiled by Franz Fassbender

Divine Love
Compiled by Franz Fassbender

Five Dream
by Sri Aurobindo

A Vision
Compiled by Franz Fassbender

Passage to More than India
by Dick Batstone

The Mother on Japan
Compiled by Franz Fassbender

Children of Change: A Spiritual Pilgrimage
by Amrit (Howard Shoji Iriyama)

Memories of Auroville - told by early Aurovilians
by Janet Feran

The Journeying Years
by Dianna Bowler

Auroville Reflected
by Bindu Mohanty

Finding the Psychic Being
by Loretta Shartsis

The Teachings of Flowers
The Life and Work of the Mother of the Sri Aurobindo Ashram
by Loretta Shartsis

The Supramental Transformation
by Loretta Shartsis

**The Mother's Yoga - 1956-1973 (English & French)
Vol. 1, 1956-1967 & Vol. 2, 1968-1973**
by Loretta Shartsis

Antithesis of Yoga
by Jocelyn Janaka

Bougainvilleas PROTECTION
by Narad (Richard Eggenberger), Nilisha Mehta

Crossroad The New Humanity
by Paulette Hadnagy

Die Praxis Des Integralen Yoga
by M. P. Pandit

The Way of the Sunlit Path
by William Sullivan

Wildlife great and small of India's Coromandel
by Tim Wrey

A New Education With A Soul
by Marguerite Smithwhite

Featured Titles

Divine Love

The texts presented in this book are selected from the Mother and Sri Aurobindo.

"Awakened to the meaning of my heart. That to feel love and oneness is to live. And this the magic of our golden change, is all the truth I know or seek, O sage."

Sri Aurobindo, Savitri, Book XII, Epilog

A Vision by the Mother

On 28th May 1958, the Mother recounted a vision she once had of a wonderful Being of Love and Consciousness, emanated from the Supreme Origin and projected directly into the Inconscient so that the creation would gradually awaken to the Supramental Consciousness. The Mother's account of this vision was brought out a first time in November 1906, in the Revue Cosmique, a monthly review published in Paris.

A Dream – Aims and Ideals of Auroville
the Mother on Auroville

50 years of Auroville from 28.02.1968 - 28.02.2018

Today, information about Auroville is abundant. Many people try to make meaning out of Auroville – about its conception, to what direction should we grow towards, and, what are we doing here?

But what was Mother's original Dream and what was her Vision for Auroville back then?

Matrimandir Talks by the Mother

This book presents most of Mother's Matrimandir talks, including how she conceived the idea for this special concentration and meditation building in Auroville.

Memories of Auroville - Told by early Aurovilians

Memories of Auroville is a book about the very early days of Auroville based on interviews made in 1997 with Aurovilians who lived here between 1968 and 1973. The interviews presented in this book are part of a history program for newcomers that I had created with my friend, Philip Melville in 1997. The plan was to divide Auroville's history into different eras and then interview Aurovilians according to their area of knowledge. Our first section would cover the years from 1968 till 1973 when the Mother was still in her physical body.

The Way of the Sunlit Path

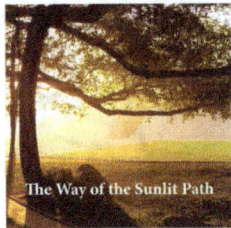

May The Way of the Sunlit Path be a convenient guide for activating this ancient truth as a support for a Conscious Evolution.

May it illumine the transformation offered to us in the Integral Yoga.

A Dream Takes Shape (in English, French, Hindi)

A comprehensive brochure on the international township of Auroville in, ranging from its Charter and "Why Auroville?" to the plan of the township, the central Matrimandir, the national pavilions and residences, to working groups, the economy, making visits, how to join, its relationship to the Sri Aurobindo Ashram, and its key role in the future of the world. This brochure endeavours to highlight how The Mother envisioned Auroville from its inception, some of the major achievements realised over the years, and some of the difficulties currently faced in implementing the guidelines which she gave.

Mother on Japan

I had everything to learn in Japan. For four years, from an artistic point of view, I lived from wonder to wonder. And everything in this city, in this country, from beginning to end, gives you the impression of impermanence, of the unexpected, the exceptional... ...everything in this city, in this country, from beginning to end, gives you the impression of impermanence, of the unexpected, the exceptional. You always come to things you did not expect; you want to find them again and they are lost – they have made something else which is equally charming.

Auroville Reflected

On 28 February 1968, on an impoverished plateau on the Coromandel Coast of South India, about 4,000 people from around the world gathered for a most unusual inauguration. Handfuls of soil from the countries of the world were mixed together as a symbol of human unity. Why did Indira Gandhi, the erstwhile Prime Minister of India, support this development for "a city the earth needs?" Why did UNESCO endorse this project? Why does the Dalai Lama continue to be involved in the project? What led anthropologist Margaret Mead to insist that records must be kept of its progress? Why did both historian William Irwin Thompson and United Nations representative Robert Muller note that this social experiment may be a breakthrough for humanity even as critics commented, "it is an impossible dream"?

A House For the Third Millennium
Essays on Matrimandir

Nightwatch at the Matrimandir...
A cosmic spectacle; the black expanse above, the big black crater of Matrimandir's excavation carved deep into the soil. The four pillars - two of which are completed and the other two nearing completion - are four huge ships coming together from the four corners of the earth to meet at this pro propitious spot...

Passage to More than India

This book is a voyage of discovery. In 1959 the author, Dick Batstone, a classically educated bookseller in England, with a Christian background, comes across a life of the great Indian polymath Sri Aurobindo, though a series of apparently fortuitous circumstances. A meeting in Durham, England, leads him to a determination to get to the Sri Aurobindo Ashram in Pondicherry, a former French territory south of Madras.